Prior poetry collections by the author:

Ripples on the Surface
Child of the Universe

Novels by the author:

Deception Past
Dragonfly Dreams
Five Flowers

Author's website: www.ReincarnationBooks.com

Author's blog: www.DeceptionPast.WordPress.com

Author's Twitter: @FrankideMerle

A CALL TO CONTEMPLATION

By

Franki deMerle

For Marta with love and gratitude

553.

I'm chasing the rainbow
The light is inside
And all around
But I can't ever hold it

Nothing I want in life is concrete
I live in vibration of light and sound
But I can't ever own it
I can't tie it down

I'm chasing the incense
Sweet scent elusive
And all around
Can't you just smell it?

Nothing I live for is material
I live in vibration of light and sound
But I can't ever sell it
I can't pin it down

I live in my dreams
Where life is for love
And love is reality

But I keep being wakened
By a harsh society
That doesn't understand

My musical mystery
My mystical flowering
Of understanding

*

554.

Are opposites alike?
Is autism the same
As addictive video gaming?
How closely related
Are stupidity and sociopathology?
Why study the inane?
To understand life
We must realize
We are alive
And go quietly inside
To observe and
Meditate

*

555.

We are the rainbow
Together the sun
Come back together as one
All it takes is more love

Who was the rainbow
Now the sun
Joined together as one
In love

All the waves of humanity
Fear, laughter and cruelty
Are just divisions of love
The prism fissions us

Hands of light
Hands of time
Make puppets of our lives
Love removes the prism illusion
One heart, one love, one mind

We can live together
We can love each other
We can tune ourselves
Into the same vibration

*

556.

The gift of words to express thought
The gift of thought to understand feelings
The gift of emotions that binds us together
The gift of alternate perception—
To understand one another
Without those life is an empty shell
Bodily functions and insecurity
A terrible aloneness
In a vibrant sea
Understanding begins
With feeling

*

557.

Be gentle with me
I trust you with my thoughts
I want to feel part of the whole
The world's a mess of misunderstanding
Come in out of the cold
Sing me your song
I want the world to know

I want to give up living prisms
I want the world to be whole
What's the point of seeing visions
If you can't touch the gold?

I've seen your private dreams
There are no secrets between us
Break the chains of fear and fly free

Light crept down upon a planet
And split into a splintered rainbow
All the people living
Fissioned from their home

If two colors blend together
Will the rainbow disappear?
The illusion is confusing
But you are really here

Light crept down into my darkness
You arrived in brilliant color
And all your splendor
Too sweet to ignore

It seems crazy to be alone
With no one else inside
Like the rainbow simply dies
Instead of turning into gold

*

558.

Travelers all
We are particles of time
Misleading ourselves
By defining what's right
Exchanging ideas
Through music and mime
Enjoy the ride
Simplify
And be kind

*

559.

Limitations open doors
Block out distractions
Keep us to our chosen path
Before we ever arrive

Obstacles need not be frustrating
Water flows around
Ignores the object of contention
Water in us abounds

*

560.

Picture me beside you now
I can touch your breath
As the earth goes spinning around
You're with me and yet
Time has closed its door
Open it, my friend

Picture me beside you now
Gently we caress
All the stars above us now
Sharing all of space

Shine the light upon the path
Help me find my way
Picture me beside you now
I see you here this way

See me deep inside your heart
Yes, you know it's true
That you're here within my heart
And I think of you
Time has tired your eyes
Now we see the truth

Picture me beside you now
Gently we caress
All the stars around us now
In their net of lace

*

561.

The Universe cannot be sculpted
The face of its creator
Cannot be depicted
To accuse blasphemers
Of the impossible
Is to reveal
One's lack of belief

*

562.

Meet me on the mountain
We'll watch the sunlight fade
Spinning among the stars
We can take our time right there
Spinning among the stars

Gentle flower in a world of thorns
You are the rainbow in my eye
Don't ever think that you're alone
We'll sow your seeds in the sky

Silent teardrop from a cloud
Swim through the river of time
It's impossible for you to drown
We'll drift back up to the sky

Straight from the heart
Our love's blood flows
Right from the start
We both have known

The stars are but jewels
On our mountainside
That mountain is our heaven
And our home

We'll watch the sunlight come and go
We can make love in the moon's glow
Spinning among the stars
Let the beauty flow

*

563.

Energy of one being crystallizes
Expands as it blows apart
Snowflakes fall

*

564.

The world is lonely
What do I know?
Silence answers for tomorrow
I am lonely
Where do I go?

Butterflies can't live in a cage
Fish can't swim on a string
And if I set you free
Will you still fly with me?

Should I stand still
What shall I do?
Silence answers for you
Outside there's nothing to do

All the people on the earth
All are by themselves
Why such silence in your heart?
Tell me what you've felt

All my thoughts
All my words
Someone hold me near

*

565.

Tired of delusions
Tired of lies
Hate cannot
Negate kindness

*

566.

All creation seems so lonely
If only we could share our pain
Our love, our dreams, our thoughts, our feelings
I want to share it all today

If we could cross that barrier
Where I am me and you are you
The fear would simply disappear
If only I could join with you

We live inside a two-room house
The door between's been closed
For such a very long time
There is one within and one without
One is faith
The other's doubt

We are awake and we are dreams
And each designs the other being
Multidimensional mirror image
Let's take that door right off its hinges

Every being's so alone
If only we could share our pain
Our love, our dreams, our thoughts, our hopes
I want to share it all today

If we could cross that barrier
Where I'm just me and you're just you
Then fear would simply disappear
If only I could share with you

Beyond the shadow and the light
A door's been open silently
For such a long, long time
We are low and we are high
There is death and there is sky

We are awake and we are knowing
We've kept the dream alive and growing
Reality's created on the other side
But we've captured the key and kept on going

All creation seems so lonely
If only we could share our pain
Our love, our thoughts, our dreams, our joy
I want to share it all today

If we could cross that barrier
Where I'm just me and you're just you
Then fear would simply disappear
And I could give myself to you

*

567. Emily

Her face mirrors mine—
What I see in the mirror
Backwards asymmetry of eyes

And the lips meet
To hide behind them
The space between two teeth

A Call to Contemplation

Now I've contemplated
All I intended
Come full circle

Back in my quiet space
A peaceful garden
A place to create

I withdraw once more
From the chaos and strife
Into the peaceful night

*

568.

The night is long
But never stays
When things go wrong
They always change

If things are wrong
Just wait for right
We need the dark
To see the light

No one knows
Which way to go
Follow your heart
Or follow your nose

We all end up
The same in the end
When all is done
We start again

Wait long enough
Night turns to day
When things are bad
They always change

Enjoy the moment
It's all we've got
The people that glow
And the ones not so hot

Everyone you know
Is as much in the dark
So before you go
Count the stars

*

569.

Poems come where feelings arise
Never confined just to write
So many tell so many lies
To create false history
But I have memory

*

570.

It's easy to lose track of time
We get so busy it just slips away
Senses dim, energy fades
Wondering when time slipped away

A Call to Contemplation

Every time we make a mistake
We get the chance to make a change
"I screwed up"
Is all you have to say

Leaders do it all the time
It doesn't matter what words are used
We hate to catch them in a lie
If only they'd just tell the truth

Nothing human, nothing gained
We're all just learning anyway
So much pleasure mixed with pain
Nothing human, nothing gained

*

571.

Sparkling silver-white air
Warmth that carries me above
Into the abyss of love

*

572.

I no longer care for lengthy speech
I have said enough
Simply let peace flow through me—
A messenger of kindness and love

*

573.

Drama teaches lessons
In literature and entertainment
Not advisable for successful relationships

Destroyer of families
Self-centeredness is cold
Kindness warms the heart

Selfishness disrupts
Compassion simplifies art
Business is not to be confused with people

Life requires honest caring
Expressions of concern and care
Acts of kindness dare

Defy cold confrontation
Drama in real life is egocentric
Void of true compassion

*

574.

Harmonious
Artful
Rich in culture
Playful

*

575.

Simplicity is attractive
And yet eventually
Are added layers of complexity

Deal with what you understand
And don't fear its kin
If you seek to destroy everything complex
To seek the world to begin again

Break the complex down in layers
Find the simple core
No need for anger or frustration
Stay with simple
No need for more

*

576.

The love of a furred or feathered friend
Never disappoints like family
Totally reliable versus thoughtless
I prefer animal company
One must never be thoughtless of them
They perceive truth in friends
But once the bond is formed
And trust established
More faithful love was never born

*

577.

Silver-haired children
Have learned there's no need
For dogma or rigid schedules

Silver-haired children
Have learned they can laugh
In the midst of disasters

Silver-haired children
Have learned not to want
Whatever they truly don't need

Silver-haired children
Have learned that opinions
Are no more than a hill of beans

*

578.

Gently strummed
Undulating wood
In accompaniment enjoyed or
Totally on its own
A solo or sung with
Rhythm its heritage

*

579.

Feelings include being hurt
Choose to believe it's unintentional
Accept what is and be peaceful
Forgive but you don't have to say so

*

580.

Liberty in the United States
Allows the crazy to be free
And frees the crazies—
Just a side-effect of liberty

Being born doesn't entitle one
To anything

*

581. for James

Strangers are more polite
Than some relations
Healthy minds exchange ideas
And pleasant wishes

But those trapped in themselves
Live in delusion, hate and lies
And don't see those around them
Offering to share kindness

We wonder how it happens
When such a lost soul breaks
And spreads his hate with weapons
In a public killing spree

Why didn't anyone see?
Well, I have seen
I cannot reason with hate
Delusion doesn't communicate

Kind offers are refused
What else can I do
He doesn't ask for help
He says he's always right

Unless he's caught breaking a law
I cannot protect innocent life
I'm grateful I didn't raise him
I'm glad he'll not stay in my life

But I wish for synchronistic intervention
To teach him how to be kind
I wish him kindness

*

582.

Happiness is a simple life
Of peace, good will and kindness
I am grateful for mine

And for this opportunity to write
The thoughts I wish to share
My ultimate expression of life

A chance to heal
A chance to learn
A chance to be still

*

583.

Gentle snowflakes
Stick to soft moss
Line tree branches
Bring in a hush

The crispness of cold
Makes faces smile
The pure precious flakes
Quiet all guile

The world is at peace
In the moment
Hibernating in freeze
Softly quiet

*

584.

Some scheme and lie
No one knows why
Or really cares

So much truth to be discerned
From this mysterious world
We help each other find

Random acts of kindness
Give meaning to aliveness
There's company in beauty

Anger wastes energy
And it's unpleasant
Who needs it?

Seek joy in mystery
Awe in beauty
Truth in being kind

*

585.

Winter hibernation
Most wish for spring
Let it come in its time
I enjoy this peace

Most wish for lost youth
Not me—I dread its return
Indiscretions, inhibitions
Ignorance, rejection

No desire to be taunted
Bullied or hated
Wondering why suffering
Must be animated

Siva gives and takes
Siva the destroyer
While Vishnu sleeps
I wait for the creator

The US survived two world wars
Before it lost faith
To even the score
Put God in his place

Preachers preach to teach themselves
One need not speak to trust someone else
Values are true currency
God's been demoted to money

Strife is everywhere
Youth worries in the dark
Experience is a comfort
That lets you trust your heart

*

586.

A mind divorced from Nature
Until a cat curls in its lap
And body provides the cure

*

587.

My most precious quality
Is the habit of learning
Delight in self-teaching—
Voyage of discovery

The more I've learned
The more patterns
Have become apparent
Patterns of life

Maps to guide through time
Orchestrated light
Reveals the pattern of patterns
That guides us through life

*

588.

On the surface
Four directions
Where really are six
Dig deep or climb
Descend or ascend
Beginning to end

Franki deMerle

Riding the waves
The storms and winds
Exposed to the sun
Cycling over again
So much is below
So much to know

So many layers
So many illusions
Feelings and colors
Of many emotions
Bottled cause damage
Undiscovered catastrophic

Stillness doesn't grasp
Agitation clings
Motion is gravity
Neutrinos pass
Through everything
You cannot hold

What matters most
But your awareness
Can choose to grow

*

589.

Stars are few
In the rainforest
Giant trees shelter

Rain water filtered
Through canopy needles
Of firs and cedars

Such abundance
Taken for granted
Water of life

A Call to Contemplation

Oxygen
Unpolluted
Aromatic

"Don't move up there
It rains all the time
You won't see the sky"

I like it just fine
I feel alive
And connected to life

Balance
Temperance
Moderation

Wind and water
Provide power
Energy sustainability

*

590.

Somewhere in my room at night
A cat softly snores
Under my bed?
In the closet?
Hiding place best undisturbed

Sometimes in my bed at night
My face is cuddled by black and white
My feet are kept warm by a sleeping giant
Safe together in the night
Warm and comfy cozy

*

23

591.

"Failure to thrive"
This is a difficult life
Made more so by bad choices

So many die
Who only dreamed to care
But never found a life

How have so many
Sunk into suffering
Forgetting there's so much more?

A color spectrum of feelings
A palette of emotions
Dulled into despair
Traded in false promise
Angry advertising
Hate knows no success

Open the heart
Accept diversity
A fresh start

Wonder and joy
At the simplest things
Make my heart sing

*

592.

The rain clears the air
In the quiet of the night
All I hear is water
Its touch is soft and light

The cleansing that it brings
Cools emotional fires
Softens the very earth
Cries for those expired
Rest for all beings

Questions unanswered
Wait to be inspired
Beings disembodied
Wait to inspire

I seek comfort
But surprise revives
Rely on habit
But routine is dying

The tiny drops make contact
Until I'm soaking wet
A marvel unexpected
That brings the wonder back

*

593.

Countless people
Seven billion
Here at once

Kapilina
We remember
Welcoming

Some aren't forgiving
So much left to learn
Still so much fighting

Now we see the differences
Now we see the damages
Misunderstanding references

Taking sides on a wheel
Turning—constant spills
Some prefer to be still

Countless stars
Share the sky
Mark the time

Kapilina
Come back together
Old hate doesn't matter

*

594.

Beauty in wind
Swaying of limbs
Dancing trees
Rhythmic breeze

Even at night
Spirit takes flight
Free in the stars
With open heart

Mind rules brain
More than we claim
Body's just a form
Beyond is an open door

Where wind blows free
Dancing with trees
And rising above
In the stars making love

*

595.

The habit of worry can make you sick
Been there, done that
Had enough of it

But sometimes you just need to cry it out
Wash away
All the false doubts

You've made it this far
So you've done something right
Sleep and let your brain take over tonight

*

596.

Times are hard for everyone
Sometimes things must be undone
I don't like my poetry edited
So I used a self-publisher

But they overcharged for sales
While royalties were slim
So I found someone else
To reverse the trend

I'm fortunate in this economy
To have a pension is comforting
Not everyone is so lucky
So a retired teacher gets my royalties

And so the three books I published first
Cost more than Kat Moran's two
But second editions will be coming soon
So they will cost less too

*

597.

This is a time to celebrate
The beginning of a new age
Souls have returned to reclaim
Their lives of the past

We are here to shed light
We are here to share truth
To remove superstitious
False ideas

To remove fear
No more need for secrets
Open hearts are free of burdens
No more guilt or shame

A time to heal the planet
Openness needs no weapon
Light a candle for yourself
And find your true path

*

598.

A fresh start
Is all anyone wants
I want openness
No secrets
No violence
No weapons
A chance to study uninterrupted
By war or riots
Or religious prejudice
A chance to be me
Openly

*

599.

If electric civilization crashes
The homeless will survive us
We're no different as humans
But the meek will live beyond us

In any confrontation
The fighters are not the survivors
Just dead and walking wounded
And the bystanders

This planet is the school of life
Where we come to breathe
Those who ignore the breath
Leave

There is no deeper meaning
No well hidden secret
Everyone living
Is doing it

A study in dark and light
We take our metaphors seriously
But the only right
Is to breathe

*

600.

We carry pain like baggage
After trauma
Physical or mental doesn't matter
It's the cause
We must revisit to heal
Physical or mental—it's all pain
Wounds that hurt
And when we hurt
We hurt others
Physically or mentally doesn't matter
If we know we can let go
Of what hurts
We must remember

*

601.

Those who need an audience
Who feel they must be heard
Have been denied

I don't enjoy center stage
I've never liked the spotlight
But I was left outside

Felt I had to prove myself
Never feeling good enough
Needing to be loved

I know it's all illusion
So trivial and unimportant
But I've cried

And none of it matters
Till it happens to you
And that's life

Some collect facts
Some search for truth
Some just try

We can accept
We can tolerate
We can be kind

*

602.

What are we made of
All living creatures
Together on this planet
Enter the waterkeepers
Ready to protect us
Keepers of our being
Ever watching
Each reporting
Polluters of our living
Ever ready to clean
Refuse from our drinking
Standing as our guardians

Help the waterkeepers
Protecting all of life
From human polluters
Watchers of our wastefulness
Protectors of the waters

*

603.

There is sadness in being forgotten
There is nothing to be done
Except remember

Some take emotion with them
Where they go
Others take their memory
It's not for me to know
Why so many are angry

The most emotive accuse others
Through projection
And never see themselves
In the mirror

They will not remember
Those who don't know themselves
Anger erases memory
Poisons the well

I drink clean water
Breathe fresh air
Remember and care

*

604.

Money may be convenient
But our bodies are mostly water
We should seek survival first

*

605.

Wasteful living produces garbage
Lack of focus causes worries
I want my remains to be recycled
No focal burial point taking up space

But there are islands in the oceans
Continents of trash and plastic
Killing life
Tipping the balance

All from wasteful living
From not paying attention
To what we're doing
To the body of this planet

We are awakening
Realization can't come too late
The waste can't be argued away
More garbage in the arguing

*

606.

Stress is contagious
So is peace
We're all connected

Emotions spread
The more they're repressed
Let's be kind instead

*

607

Humans are animals
Animals feel and perceive
We all have needs
Domestic pets are family
They need love and validation too
Those who are cruel
Those who ignore or neglect
Are soulless fools

It's so easy to care
It's so natural to love
We're programmed to share
Having anything is enough

How many times I needed a friend
And a bird or a cat or a dog was there
Listening with concern in their eyes
Letting me know they care

The least we can do is be kind to them
People domesticated them
They've so much love to share
All we need do is care

*

608

Fog clouds in
Shrouds the night
In mystery

Temperature drops
Fog turns to ice
Crystalline beauty

Cold slows everything down
Stills all worldly vibrations
And leaves an ice painting

*

609.

I'm not afraid to be alone
I've always known this time would come
Not everyone we know and love
Is embodied

The veil is thin
We come and go
Across the threshold
Of time

And those I love are always here
Even when they can't be here
We often reach across the boundary
And touch

*

610

Creativity cannot be produced on demand
Love should not be dismissed out of hand
But anger knows no reason
Anger is not rational
And never understands

*

611.

Some people come to party
Some to socialize
Some are all about money
Some want to live active lives

I just want peace and quiet
And freedom to be myself
I don't need politics
I've nothing to prove

I write letters to the universe
I don't know who will read them
I don't care what they think
But I'm grateful for responses
They take the time to make

When one enters life
With a talent in one's hand
One needn't search for purpose
That life is already planned

I'm grateful for my ability
Self-expression builds confidence
It's led me on a journey
To a source of my own competence

And I appreciate others
Finding and following their gifts
They've found their own lives' paths
Treasures through which others sift

*

612.

Our input comes from physical senses
I delight in simple pleasures
A sweet smell
A tasty morsel
A bath in warm water
A caress

Even pain observed becomes a joy
With realization of living nerves
Observe and transform into harmony

*

613.

Mercurial energy passes
Dreams illuminate the way
If it upsets the gut don't do it
Live in the moment
Make it last
Slow down and stay

The only difference I need to make
Is inside me
In the way I approach and perceive
Nature will take care of the rest
I've nothing to prove or believe
It is what it is
Just observe and breathe

*

614.

The more people on earth
The greater number
Of variants
Of violence

It's an interesting party
Watch the suffering
Multiply
Because suffering is what most live by

Everyone thinks their problems are worst
When they don't see the whole picture
I'll take my own problems any day
It's never as hard as it's been

Emotions make short memories
Or faulty ones at best
But who is not at fault for something?
We can only do our best

Let it go
Forgive
But don't forget
Memory's our only defense

*

615.

Those who have no love
For loving pets
Are not enough
To hold my interest

Clueless
One who ignores
Unconditional love's source

Stay away from my door
My pets are so much more
To me and the universe
I need say no more

*

616.

This is the age of opinions
Where everyone has something to say
This is the Age of Aquarius
Where together we bring about change

Thinkers are welcome
Compassion much needed
The youth must awake
And arise

This isn't the time to hack computers
Or scapegoat those you don't like
Now has a place for everyone
At the universal table

We consume this planet together
We must all play a part in survival
Cooperation is the imperative
Compassion must be the true motive

*

617.

Sea foam
Like an ice cream float
An acidic drink
A carbonated beverage

The ocean is acidic
The sea is carbonated
And ice calves fall everyday

What we are seeing
Is a tide turning
A wave not going our way

Or maybe dessert
After consuming the planet
A tab for someone to pay
And clean up the table

*

618.

Sociopaths excited by pain
Are sadists with different brains
From compassionate beings

Is their purpose to teach us balance
Or outrage?

They think themselves superior
To genuine human beings
They think without reason or consequence

I think them simply ignorant
Of life

*

619.

What we don't understand
Is deified
All we can comprehend
Is minute

Compared to the vastness
Of what is
We process patterns
To begin

We look into the microscope
We look into the mirror
We look out through the telescope
We see the basic error

Reflection
Versus outside looking in
Projection
Versus inside looking out

We question
We doubt
We struggle with guilt
For faith disproven

Nature versus nurture
Nature's nature is to nurture
Nurturing is natural
The natural world is internal

It's all very simple
Learn about consequences
And do whatever happens
To make you happy

*

620.

Everyone feels they have a purpose
Everyone has a gift
A talent with which one is born
One's natural usefulness
Never should be ignored

*

621.

Slowing down
Out of the rat race
Time to listen

A breeze in the trees
The brush of a whisker
And a purr

Bodily warmth
Comfort hug
Snuggles close

I am loved

*

622.

A planet sighs and heaves
An infestation raises temp
Poisons its fluids with no relief
The Earth is sick

She is an ecology
Unto herself
We are virology
Attacking her wealth

Franki deMerle

She has defenses
She will survive
But will we, her children,
Have to die

Or start over again in humility
In balanced small communities
Practicing sustainability

Focus on the bigger picture
Many destroy us all
"We" are more than human beings
"We" must include all of Earth

The pettiness of egos
Is microbiology
So much beyond a body to know
Squandered in self pity

The Earth will survive
But we are alive now
And now is not the time
To fight

*

623.

What's the point of music
Without harmony?
What's the point of rhythm
Without melody?

A Call to Contemplation

What's the point of all the noise
Blaring throughout society?
Except to make us sick
By drowning out our humanity

Listen to the stars
Starlight is quiet

Listen to the bubbling brook
The surging surf
The winter wind
Listen to your breath

*

624.

Age gives perspective
That youth cannot know
The fresh taste of juice
Becomes fine Bordeaux

Give it a rest
Rehearsed worries
Become impressed
With whom you will be

Taking one's time
Is not a vice
Being thick skinned
Isn't kind

Politics are for those willing to fight
I seek no more drama
I hold peace in mind
And accept the flow of time

*

625.

When I was a child she hated me
The games she played always ended in pain
But the child always believes her mother
However big the lie

And hers were full of morbid detail
Vulgar fabrications
To fill my small head with nightmares
Painted by her fear

My mother was crazy
And no one cared enough to tell me
My mother hated me
But there was no one there to save me

And so I am alone
Life is disconnected—
The people not the flow—
Connections break

Just when I think
I've touched someone
They go

I wanted to talk so I called my Dad
Turns out he didn't know
Ironic I'm now the age he was
When I was born

*

626.

Death, familiar visitor
When will you come for me
And take me from this burdensome
Habit of misery—
Death is unreliable
Instead I'll count on sleep

*

627.

Yes-but is the ultimate
In frustration construction
Someone goes from crisis to crisis
Because they're afraid to be left alone
Leave me in peace!

Yes-but doesn't see the present
Lives in a climate of the past
Someone goes backwards projecting
Because they're afraid to let go—
Let go of me!

*

628.

My dreams have been under siege for decades
Why should I welcome another year?
The world is a mass production
And I'm not in the big picture

It's like I'm in the way
I dream my dreams and the world sees the need
For ethnic cleansing
Erase the misfit thought

And I'm the impurity
Because so few look at what's here
And see what is actually here

*

629.

As soon as the light is sought
The shadow speaks its heart
And I cannot tell its voice apart
From myself

*

630.

As I grew my vision blurred
Such fuzziness to sort out
Groping for light and direction
There was so much to wonder about

If I could see clearly
I wouldn't have to ask
But lacking sensibility
I just sit back and laugh

*

631.

She measured everything
As if following
A recipe

Noting each painstakingly
Quart to pinch to spoon
Measuring

And when the meal was finished
And all were satisfied
She picked it all apart with pride

She would not give—
Could not let go
Love died

*

632.

Poetry consists of finite lines
Its essence is just
One day at a time

*

633.

Men who've always slept alone
Celibate and cold
Believe that women must be told
How to nurture their fold

What the fuck?
Seriously?
Society progresses
But clergy don't respect us

Women of faith in themselves
Know better than to listen
To such absurdity

Priests worship an alleged virgin
Who no doubt had many children
And dealt with reality

But what about the young?
What about the naïve?
False belief destroys clarity

Centuries have passed
But male clergy still try
To control and manipulate
Womankind—enough already!

*

634.

Many angry people are afraid
They can't control life's changes
They're frustrated by what they don't understand
So they hate

It's a nebulous hate
Based on misinformation
And fear of change
And fear of differences

They impose misery on others—
Their grief over feeling inadequate
To understand and carry on
Life's pace as outrun them

And I know because I've been overwhelmed
Felt I couldn't go on
But did for those by whom I was loved
I moved on

And all we need to do is slow down
And meet life on friendly terms
No one hates a slower pace
But no one loves the hate

*

635.

Respect is an aspect of love
Love offered without is a lie
When war is thought a necessity
Respect has died

Many cultures are close to empty
Running on fumes of memories
But when war is thought necessary
Hope has died

*

636.

Clutter, waste, trash, debris
Too many people
Too many things

Learn from Nature
Not from man
Live as simply as you can

I have possessions
Mementos of friends
I keep because I miss them

Franki deMerle

It's hard to let go of beauty
It's hard to keep space free
It's hard to let go

But simplicity leads
To happiness
While money causes greed

It's hard to let go of feelings
It's hard to let go of the past
But we must to live in the present

So hard to face the dealings
That have brought me to where I am
Look and let go—move on again
Simplicity

*

637.

The dreaded big A
Slow death of the brain
Forced to face the truth
We're not the geniuses we presumed

We lose the future and the past
And have only the present moment
And all around us
Is seen through fresh eyes

The pain of slow fade
The loss of names
The end is relief to all
We grieved throughout it all

A Call to Contemplation

And all let go so easily
Nightmares of having to repeat
An ordeal we could not control
Let go

*

638.

Everyone's cursed with a family
Some are fortunate instead
When family focuses on possessions
They'll all be ungrateful when you're dead

Some choose not to be sociable
Afflicted with deficiency of love
Some think everyone a bother
An interference they wish were gone

Everyone chooses who they are
I don't want to live without love
Acknowledgement is required to be part of my life
And manners but not possessions

I'm lucky to have found family outside of blood
Choice is a self-allowed luxury
To know who you trust
And set priorities

I'm grateful now for no children
I see others' heartache of disappointment
Which reflects upon themselves
And lack of communication

But what is the point of holding a grudge?
Forgiveness sheds the burden
Does not imply safe trust
It leaves you free to love

*

639.

Others try to tell me
I must do things their way
No way—leave me be

My preferences do not conform
Simplicity isn't the norm
It's not good commercial form

But I am simple
It's how I perceive
Nature as a temple

I follow my path
I don't care to wander
It's my chosen task

Rejection of another's ways
Is not rejection of them
But acceptance of diversity

*

640.

Emotional adults have patience
They wait for the time to be right
So much in life is about timing
Wine doesn't mature overnight

I used to want everything now
But I learned as I grew to slow down
If the wine isn't ready
Don't pour it out

Hopes become unrealistic expectations
I know the let down well
I learned to temper my impatience
To wait for the silent bell

*

641.

Much pain is the price of sensitivity
And seeing what lies deep inside
Rarely do others share this gift
To suffer in order to know the sublime—
An inspiration to forgive

*

642.

What is it that defines us?
We analyze the pieces
Evaluate percentages
Try to see the whole—

It's never there
What is it we are seeking?
What is it that completes us?
What adventure must we dare?

We look into the mirror
But it isn't there
And that is what we're seeking—
The piece that isn't there

That is how to read us
That is how to see the whole
By finding the missing part
That is how we know

*

643.

We've much in common
But I've discarded much
Burdens become so heavy

I don't like being weighed down
The pressure is too much
And so I strive for levity

My brain has trouble coping
I've learned ways to handle such
Options are opportunities

It helps to see the patterns
And break them when one must
It helps to see possibilities

I talk to the Universe
Whenever I'm depressed
It never hides from me

I can count on galaxies
To always be there for me
Unlike many people

The stars are my support group
Animals, flowers, trees
The sun and moon are here for me

They show me many patterns
And have earned my trust
For options—infinity

*

644.

I am a wordsmith
Explorer of the heart
I'm at home within
I embrace both light and dark

Wary of perfection
I know does not exist
I live in the world of natures
The point is that I live

I'm not a part of business
Or science or religion
I am appalled at politics
Toying with living beings

I don't need wars or weapons
Because I have my words
I trust them to explain me
Regardless if I'm heard

I am a puzzle solver
A riddler at some times
I understand the depth of dreams
I travel the tome of time

Mostly I seek laughter—
To understand the puns
That language plays upon our brains
Living should be fun

I'm not much for rules
They only get in my way
I see no need for protocol
To simply stage my play

For all that nonsense causes pain
And stress and tears to flow
And so I dance my mercurial way
To wherever I may go

I leave behind a poem or two
And hope you will enjoy
Mystic mysteries written into
The words that I employ

*

645.

When our bodies die
They find another
I remember

*

646.

In many ways I am naïve
But not so much as some
Who do not examine what they believe
Sending logic on the run

In superstitious times gone by
Many myths were told
Stories rich in metaphor
Belied by trace of bones

The message lost in literal terms
Common sense as well
For skin and bone return to earth
The mortal being's shell

Believe as you may but fairy tales
Will take you by surprise
One day you'll awake without yourself
And see without your eyes

*

647.

Flowers are chemistry
Botany communicates
Plants can read

They see the world around them
And use it to work wisdom
Who else can live on light?

We cannot live without them
We should be listening to them
For they can speak

We hear them through our noses
They touch us through our eyes
And communicate in dreams

*

648.

Bugs have many reasons
Messengers by nature
They notice what we fail to see
They point out our inanity
And help us keep our memory
And when our bodies fail
Bugs recycle
And make our garbage useful
A sting, a bite—
Unsubtle reminders
Of what we left behind

*

649.

Humans are Nature's clowns
But when we take ourselves seriously
We let ourselves down

*

650.

Once we hunted and gathered
And then we tasted wine
And now it seems all that we do
Is advertise

*

651.

Koi—silver, gold
Flaming orange
The real McCoys
And anything but

Language is fickle
Over time
Meanings reverse

And yet
We forget

*

652.

How does one choose to murder?
How does the wonder of life disappear?
How does one learn to hate?
I guess it starts with not caring
Or maybe betrayal
But I really don't want to know

Such a violent country I live in
Such a violent world
But I've no need to fight back
No need to engage with hate
There's always another way

The world goes on and forgets
Suicides, homicides and wars
Because there is so much more
To life

*

653.

Softness of moss
Petals float down
Like flakes of snow

Fuzzy bumblebees
Soft to the eye
Contrast with death's sting

Petals fall on moss
Contrasted by the crunch
Of feet upon pebbles

But snow is melting
Petals are falling
Breeze is blowing

In a city full of gardens
Wild forests and parks
Surrounded by mountains

Life is hard
But happiness laughs
In all that's soft

*

654.

I grew up feeling I had something to hide—
The yelling and arguing, the family fights
The world didn't look the way it appeared
I was confused for so many years

Don't talk about memories from before childhood
Don't be yourself in the neighborhood
Don't ever be seen with different colored skin
Don't let anyone know you have black kids for
        friends

A Call to Contemplation

Hide your feelings toward society's games
The fact you won't play is the source of your shame
But I never want to feel that way again
I have no more energy to pretend

Life can be simple
Honest and true
I've nothing to hide
From a world full of lies

There was no innocence in childhood for me
Because there was no simplicity
The shame wasn't mine
I have nothing to hide

The shame was wanting to be kind
Kindness has nothing to hide
Life without kindness has nothing to give
I never want to live like that again

Free from hate
Free from fears
Free from anger
Free from tears

There's no shame in feelings
There's nothing to hide
Life can be simple
Life can be kind

*

655.

I'm not a digital program
Society has strayed far
From its earthly roots
Most stray by following the crowd
Seven billion on the land

There is no digital program
For civilization's progress
Manmade religions compliment
The programming process
Politics patterns itself after them

To me it seems so masculine
Ignores the cycles of the moon
Denies our earthly roots
We can't break free too soon
Except it's inconvenient

And there we have to choose
Nature or invention
Follow the crowd
Or buck manmade rules
Depends on personal truth

I'm a child of the moon
I've no need to reproduce
For I give birth to words
And four dimensional thoughts
A terminal time on earth

Everything's temporary here
Nothing lasts
The worldwide web an electric charge
Ions freed in rolling thunder
The atmosphere will clear

*

656.

Some men like to watch others fight
Caught up in their dreams of war
They sow seeds of mistrust to divide
And believe they have conquered

Some women live to manipulate
Tie invisible strings
Pretend to be sweet and wait
Strangle then leave others dangling

People waste a lot of energy
Playing pointless games
Maybe they don't know differently
Wasting all their days

Seven billion people
I'm so alone I write
To vent the endless feeling
In simplicity is time

*

657.

Naps are sudden passageways
Into our inner selves
A chance to tune in
Defragment and set sail
Correcting the direction
And once reset and awake
There is no question

*

658.

Peacefulness of reality
Internet unplugged temporarily
Visiting with neighbors
Time at home alone

No bombardment
No off the wall opinions
No trivia of other people
In other places

Sometimes it's a wonder
To connect long distances
Mostly it's illusion
That many are friends

Here I am in my place
Here I am face to face
Life is real
And at my pace

*

659.

Sadness seeks an outlet
Support from others
Outpouring of feelings
Outpouring of tears
Of words

Without pain of the past
A poet does not write
Without pressure from within
It all remains inside
Out of sight

The house is painted yellow and blue
The trim is white
In all kinds of weather
We have sunshine
And blue skies

And flowers
Humans are in pain everywhere
So grow more flowers
Everyone needs flowers
Everyone needs to smile

I'm tired of all the suffering
Buddha tamed his mind
It takes lots of practice
It takes lots of time
I sit in time

Franki deMerle

Some take vows of silence
Stillness of tongue in peace
Some go to therapy
I pluck the strings
I seek harmony

I seek
I write
I stumble
I fall
I smile

*

660.

There is comfort in routine
An adventure in change
It's balance between the two
Life bids us embrace

As in temperate climates
The seasons take their turns
So life thrives and enjoys
Repetition helps us learn

Such is the way of Nature
Who are we to not agree
With our origins and heritage?
In balance we are free

*

661.

Some people socialize
Safe in the crowd
Some need others
To feel they have power
But those who need others
To give and care for
Are the powerful

I need solitude
Animals and flowers
Are my society
Time with crowds
Tends to drain me
I prefer gentility
Of Nature

Power's an illusion
A false sense of control
In a world of constant change
No matter what you know
Things cannot stay the same
You cannot change the change
But you can be unafraid

*

662.

Beauty is thought shallow
By those who don't know
The more beauty you find
The deeper you go

*

663.

There's salt in the air
And air in the sea
The ocean is full
Of electricity

We live on the earth
And burn calories
Breathing the air
Into watery bodies

Parts make the whole
We're the sum of our parts
Together one soul—
A community's heart

We have what we need
We grow what we eat
When we work together
Life is complete

*

664.

War disrespects life
Anger destroys from within
Funerals and goodbyes
Peace returns in the end
What was the point?

A generation goes by
And does it again
Nothing gained
Nothing learned
War happens

Because we lose focus
Vision blurs
We feel others taunt us
Even when they don't
Every time is different

We lie to ourselves
Every time's a profit
For someone else
War destroys from within
No enemy is needed

Peace need not end
If we just stay focused
On being good friends
Or making amends
Peace need not end

*

665.

Dreams of all potential
Dreams of the impossible
The brain stores it all
Imprint of the soul

*

666.

What is this image
Viewed in a mirror?
We take it for granted
Or loathe or pamper it

71

But do we listen?
Do we let it speak?
Do we look in its eyes
And truly see?

How much it can tell us
It manifests again
Our basic essence
Since time began

It must be owned
Acknowledged as true
Worn comfortably
Our infinite view

And reactions to others
Met face to face
The unconscious knows
Intuitive grace

Pay attention to dreams
Recognition is there
Familiarity seen
Viewer beware

River under the bridge
Clean or poisoned
A chance to repair
Relationships broken

Opportunity to lead
By example for some
A chance for change
So good may be done

But first know the face
Looking back at you
In deep reflection
Claim the truth

*

667.

Did you ever have a favorite villain
That history scandalized
And you always took her side
When others criticized?

And then you measured the death mask
And discovered that the size
Was very close proportionately
To the face into whose eyes
You look daily?

Denial runs deep with shame and disgrace
When you trusted so many
You deny it's your face
That others cursed to infamy
And shame

I've always defended her
Without knowing why
Others insist I'm wrong
They're so sure they know better
But she sang a lovely song

Lost in a world of intrigue
Prepared only for romantic fantasy
Could she really have been me?

Franki deMerle

Hypnotized I told a story
Not at all one from history
But one of betrayal and misunderstanding
Rape and shame and mockery
And never understanding
Why those I trusted ruined me
Why those I loved laughed at me
Even as my head was chopped off

No one heard me
Language and cultural barriers
No one listened
Because I was irrelevant
Because I was romantic
Because I was a woman

It's hard to face similarities
Of times and places and other faces
But there are no coincidences
And the unconscious tries to protect
By not saying it outright

Because I'm a woman
Over the centuries
I've learned people's deceit
Invalidation and rejection
Is their own arrogance

They took a brush and painted me
In shades of their own selves
I was naïve
I wrongly believed
What they told me

A Call to Contemplation

No wonder I seek seclusion
Try to avoid socialization
This lifetime has been yet another variation
On the theme
Well, I'm just me

The past is done
Let it be
Too many what ifs
Destroy inner peace

The present moment
Is all that's needed
Let the unconscious
Learn from memories

*

668. for Lynn Koppang

This will always be Lynn's day
A day of remembrance
Pain is ended
Sleeping peacefully

Taken from his suffering
A parent, husband and neighbor
Patriot, soldier, farmer
Such kindness to remember

*

Franki deMerle

669.

Alternate realities
The chemistry of moods
Many haven't even
The luxury of food
But the rich carry on
As if life were just a game
And science goes on
Trying to explain
The mortality it cannot end
Religion diverts attention
From this world to another
That may or may not exist
But we pretend
It's all forever

Acceleration of changes
No time to absorb
Contemplate side effects or reactions
Everything changes
But the rate of the changes
Exceeds what our brains
Can comfortably adapt to
So we break into pieces
Lives and families shatter
Countries and ways of life disintegrate
Sensibility buried in rubble
Of what we thought was real
Never again trusting of
Priorities others build

A Call to Contemplation

I only want to be at peace
Putter in the garden
Pluck the strings that sing
Of harmonies unforgotten
I want to breathe
But not forever
Just a quiet time at peace
To carry that peace with me
When I go
I will go
Without artificial means
Because only connected to Nature
Is there peace
Nature is the peace in me

Artificial pressures mount
Forcing fuels from shale
People working dirty jobs
Risking filth and hell
We rob the earth of vitals
And expect to be sustained
We must give as well as steal
It's not all ours to claim
Beauty is the gift most overlooked
By those of the fortune game
There is energy in our own brains
But we must live at peace in the zone
To sustain what matters most—
Nature's soul

*

670.

When I leave this body
I know where I'm to go
Cross the ocean north by the sea
Kirks, ships, sheep, lads, lassies and me

Seems I have a date to keep
Contract with a friend
Only hope, simplicity and grace
Take part in this ephemeral plan

Let me breathe the salty air
And meet him there
Near where he said
Days for yarns and airs

Only do what makes you happy
Don't you fret the rest
Eternity is only the moment
Seek and feel the best

All of heaven in one place
No need to wander far
Dawns and clouds of Nature's art

Take my hand and dance with me
Under the stars we are free
Natural connections allow us to breathe
Eternal moments are possibilities
Sing with me

*

671.

Those who falsely accuse
Project their guilt onto you
They'll say you're a bully
Always looking for ways
To stab them in the back
You'll feel bullied
You'll need to watch your back

You'll feel hated
And resented for being here
In the way of others
So many unresolved issues
We can only face with tears
We'll find a way

You may consider dying
To escape the hate
But you've just as much right
To stay
You'll feel trapped
But love and take care of your pets
You are temporarily trapped
In a world of war and hate and weapons

They could just ignore you
Instead of resorting to abuse
They'll waste their energy
Trying to get rid of you
Because of who you remind them of
Closed eyes in front of mirrors
You're inconvenient
Like global warming
So much wasted energy

Science has proven I have extra nerve endings
To me everyone else appears dense
But they say I'm too sensitive
So I build a wall
To protect myself
I feel I was born where I didn't belong
And I was alone
Now I yawn at hearing the same old song
I just want histrionics to leave me alone

*

672.

Politics is a power game
A delusion for thick skin
I don't know what they see in it
I see others who can't get in

Because they make sense
Because they care
About others who are outcasts
Having trouble finding fare

But I can't handle the meanness
Deceit and untruths told
The secrets they believe they keep
Like we don't know we've been sold

I'm quick to latch onto hope
To believe the promise made
And always disillusioned again
By illicit barter and trade

Of human life
For the delusion of control
Of others' minds
The wheel rolls on

*

673.

Judgmental and myopic
Always wants control
Never noticing the obvious

*

674.

Life reflects values
Values are personal truths
Not judgments
Judging wastes life

Peace is the serenity
We find at the center of being
Where we leave behind
What interrupts peace

I have left much behind
I've no intention to reclaim
The more discarded
The more is at the heart of
My life

I have always wanted to be wise
Always wondered if it were possible for me
But wisdom is found in life
As long as there is peace

*

675.

I'm growing old
Such an honor
Not everyone gets to
I've made it this far
And I'm learning to be old

I see youth—some lost
Ignorant of so much
Bombarded constantly
With no time to delve deep
Or comprehend the before
Everything out of context

In my youth there was hatred
Violence and trips to the moon
And a man of peace and faith
Shot down because he was hated
And walls and prisons and nukes

Somehow I made sense of some
And suffered through the rest
Somehow my body began to fail
And I became depressed
And now I'm old

I know I'm not alone
I avoid crowds
They wear me down
Old is just a cycle of nature
That I have found

*

676.

Neon plum in midsummer light
Ripening its way to nature's delight
Sour apples hanging in the next tree
Almost four decades of work to be seen

Where humans have learned to perpetuate
The natural craft and propagate
All food comes from nature
Whom we've learned to manipulate

Why can't we just be satisfied with that
Instead of war games and military maps?
Is history really the power track
Or the DNA record that goes all the way back

To the beginning of life?
How many forms have died
In the wake of our lies?
Can't living in peace make it right?

*

677.

It's a good life
After a sentence in hell
Working against my inner self

We're comfortable
Most of the time
With much to do, learn and find

We eat well
Locally grown
Unafraid of the unknown

It all changes
No one knows when
There is no fear in death

The natural way
The middle way
The living of each day

*

678.

We all seek safety from evil
We all want bad ways to change
Each of us suffers our individual role
Searching for an end to collective pain

Some more than others—
Deluded with self-importance and ego—
The barriers to our solutions
They don't understand the inflicted toll

It's too intense
All this violence
Anger to rage to explosions
Reject the anger

Seek a peaceful refuge
Don't contribute to the insanity
Seek calm
Be at peace

Even when suffering
Be in peace
In the midst of confusion
Be the peace

*

679.

The art of aging
Is minimizing pain
Exercise, activity
Muscles must retain
Elasticity

The art of aging
Is gentle work
Converting a body
Avoiding the inert
Or extremes

The art of aging
Is admitting you're changing
Embracing the change
While staying at ease
Gracefully

*

680.

People are in different places
I only know about mine
The accomplishments and disgraces
The little pieces I've been able to find

When someone's dealing with feelings
They project them onto you
And what in the world they're on about
You haven't got a clue

When another is living a fantasy
And you just can't see their reality
Communication's gone askew
There's little you can do

Franki deMerle

And when ignorance speaks as if it knows
You can't stop stupidity from being shown
Opinions are confused for fact
You might as well just turn your back

Someone you'd mistaken for a friend
Who lies and betrays you in the end
All along had some other agenda
Than friendship

It's just the way it is
So many humans in this world
Moving about on their own missions
It's hard to make lasting connections

Some collect acquaintances
And say they're social beings
Some of us prefer solitude
In which to dive much deeper

Families fight and families break
Torn apart by judgments and hate
We can choose to not allow
Invasion of condemnation

We cannot choose who will agree
To love us back or share our peace
But we can choose to ostracize
Those who hate the dignified

Nothing hurts more than rejection
Except betrayal
But we can leave it far behind
And choose to be peaceful

The only stipulation
Is you cannot be afraid
Of your resulting isolation
To live beyond the hate

*

681.

Wet rock
Hard surface
From the bowels of the earth
Found eons ago
Soft water
Fallen from clouds above
Ever transforming

Soft and hard
Above and below
Present and long ago
Minerals in water
Softening hard edges
Both altered by air
Together

*

682.

The fire of life
Fire in the belly of earth
Calories that burn inside
Magma that moves upward

The animation of the body
Formation of the landscape
Spirit moving flesh
Solidifying—breaking the surface

We are what we are
Part of the living earth
Coexisting in toleration
Ever changing picture

*

683.

A crush of cultures
Where there is less vegetation
Where there is less respect for difference
The cacophony explodes
Grates and irritates

The soul requires quiet
To introspect
To reflect
To become acquainted with its nature
Before it can express
Itself

*

684.

The aging body longs for rest
The comfort of the peace of death
A false promise perhaps

Once released from worn out shoes
Free to fly—free to choose
Reinvigorated again

New shoes want to run and play
Slowing down with every day
Until the wear and tear cause pain

And then the need to rest again
To think no thoughts but peaceful end
Slow down in youth to stop and listen

*

685.

Ever faster paced
Society swarms and leaves no space
Individuality seeks to escape
Resist the fads and desires and race

There is no shame in moving slow
Or traveling against the flow
For wisdom leads to happiness
And wisdom comes only from within

*

686.

So much sadness
So much tenderness
To feel is to live

The body's input comes from senses
The information is relentless
The environment has something to say

And so we feel to live
For we must listen
To understand

Only when we understand
Have we anything to give
Have we meaning in which to live

*

687.

The authentic optimist
Sees beyond money and politics
Reaches for life of substance
Reaches beyond the meanness

Does not appear pragmatic
What is realistic about avarice?
It cannot sustain a way of life
Involving peace and kindness

The person who chooses to live in fear—
For it is a choice to hate and fear—
Lives in a very small part of the brain
With room for only tears and pain

Call me foolish or unrealistic
But I have found the secret of balance
That leads to peace and happiness—
The secret of compassion

*

688.

Stones that stand
Amid pebbles raked
Manmade lines
In Nature's place

Where humans strive
To be at peace
To find what stills
To find release

Beneath the trees
So tall above
Amid the tears
From heaven fallen

Like little kisses
From afar
Heaven sent
To kiss the heart

These are places
Where we find
Ourselves

*

689.

A single red leaf
Herald of the season
Individuality—
The glory of freedom
To change when it's ready
For its own reason

*

690.

We attach ourselves to our talents
But it doesn't have to be
It's all a matter of balance

If we learn from the road we travel
We can journey further on
Without stress making us unravel

All that we have is who we are
Unexpressed by demonstration
But confidence in compilation

*

691.

My life is a call to contemplation
Seeing all from many perspectives
Finding treasures deep within

Metaphor and symbolism
Lead to many levels
Unconsciously joined in the end

Every individual manifests
The allegory of evolution
Archetypes of our dissolution

Every time I venture out
I find the mirror waiting
Reflecting what's not chosen

A call to contemplation
All that's rejected is ourself
Fear is the motivation

Only kindness can replace it
Only kindness heals the hurts
One kind in all the Universe

Rhyme is a call to notice
Rhythm underlies
Each drop in the ocean

*

692.

Just another "clever" being
Underhandedly cheating the system
Living blind to consequences
Instead of finding empathy
Even numb to feeling

How did she choose her path?
Has she consciously chosen?
Has her life been so difficult—
Her awareness down to instinct
And knee-jerk reaction?

Judgment based on labels—
Upended definitions
Living on the surface
Indifferent to deeper havens
Education by conviction

How many there are like her
Enjoying momentary pleasures
Treating others as if they owe her
Ignoring the mirror
I've been there

Just so easy to be busy
Until the pain breaks through
Learning there are no differences
In between me and you
Eventually face the truth

Haven't we caused our own circumstances?
Haven't we done this to ourselves?
Hasn't the world suffered enough
From pretending it's us and them?

*

693.

The present moment
A cat purrs softly against the sound of distant
traffic
As I'm engulfed in life processes

Life is a process
Ideas, enterprises and body functions
Interruptions bring revelations

All we have is in this moment
Though all we are exceeds the concept of time
It feels like being stranded mid-motion

Interruptions stop us in our tracks
To give us the opportunity to switch back
To our chosen path

So much happens in the moment
What attracts our attention beyond it
But the duality we live in?

Interruptions in the present moment
Are the essence of mindfulness
And awareness

You cannot find your chosen path
If you don't know where you are
In the present moment

*

694.

A life written in rhyme
Each poem a point in time
And spacial life
The dimension of emotion

The essence of creativity
All down to feeling
Expression of chemistry

The essence of being
Consciously sensitive
Sharing perspective

A window for other eyes
To see backward through time
Into my tiny life

It must be in my DNA
I can't imagine any other way
To live without the rhythm

Always demanding expression
And all my poetry
Is only what I perceive

In this moment
Does life require a record in time
Of what transpires within the mind?

Or do feelings unrequited
Seek fulfillment from other life?
Whatever the answer I'm satisfied

I find it worth my while to write
To speak to an audience I cannot see
Beyond the bright stage light

*

695.

How many stories are there to be told?
Is it egotistical to tell one's own
Or just a matter of what is best known?
Is it form or content that steals the show?

Seven billion souls alive
Every day so many die
But more are reborn
The stress takes its tithe

Some believe there is valor in violence
Some differentiate between defense and offense
I don't like all the noise and stress
So much less pain in kindness

It's all about money
It's all about pride
Neither are really
Substantial or alive

And yet in entertainment
We seek pain and drama
As if vicariously
We can humor karma

A Call to Contemplation

I see beauty in Nature
Which man tramples on
I see grace in water
As it flows around

Obstacles—dramas—with no ado
It's all upstream and water is cool
And I hope Nature has a few tricks up her sleeve
To balance our foulness and germinate seeds

The Arctic is melting
The sea level rising
Will it balance the acidity
So compromising?

No nuclear holocaust to date
That's something to celebrate
But the trigger for change initiated
When the atom was no longer safe

A quest for knowledge?
No! A quest for power
Obtuse and oblivious
As summer showers

And young adults everywhere
Embark on their quest—
A question of career
Or a question of what's best?

The question is of values—
Life or death
People or possessions—
Which is wealth?

*

696.

I came into this life to heal
From trauma done to my soul
By way of my body

It's hard to get my mind around
The violence done to me
It's hard to comprehend
Violence continually
Nonstop—a runaway train
Running over everyone

I choose a safe lifestyle
I've managed to survive
When each new issue compiles upon
The wound so deep inside

It comes down now to trust
I've set perimeters
Defined my space for safety
Because I must

So many years it takes to heal
Embracing transformation
Simply being still

And when the last poem is written
Will it be the last?
Will there be any further need
To carry on the past?

*

697.

The future loops around behind us
While we look ahead
The only thing that lies before
Is after we are dead
And then we see our past
Alive before us

So many choices
All lead to inner space
All lead to this very moment
We're meant to contemplate
And see it all as one
Past and future disintegrate

Possibilities are infinite
Must we differentiate?
Must we agitate?
Carry on as separate
Or simply sit
And integrate?

*

698.

The older I get the more I question
And what I believe no longer matters
It just is
The present flowers

*

Franki deMerle

699.

Academics see intelligence
But don't understand the creative process
So quick to analyze and categorize
And create rules that make a mess

Creativity doesn't follow rules
It knows what it does best
Nature plus infinity
Is the answer to the test

Academics see details
Oh they may see the big picture as well
But they must narrow focus
To publish and sell

Maybe in retirement
They step back and realize
The fallacy of tunnel vision
In details are the lies

So many possibilities
And no need to decide
Because it all leads to
The sum of all of life

*

700.

My country values ignorance
Control is called success
Change is inevitable

Children bullied for their brains
Politicians making claims
Without intention

100

I pity the "rich"
They've so little time
To find happiness

All around stupidity
Has replaced integrity
But it will change

*

701.

We share our lives
As gifts to each other
I share thoughts in writing
For whatever others
Choose to share by reading

How else would I try
To touch many?
I'm rarely noticed otherwise
Out of step with time and technology
No interest in popularity

The games people play for attention
Cause them to be someone else
Or else I'm just not like them
I play rhymes with myself
But give up no true intention

Politics drains away energy
From improving one's integrity
Popularity is merely façade of love
And hinders self-discovery
I am true solitary

The need to be loved
Is strong enough
To drive one to costumes
And cover-ups
Just to attract illusion

The need to be loved
Should push one to reveal
Just who one is
And show what one feels
To all existence

It's the only way
For the love you seek
To find you

*

702. To Al Franken

Tis the week before Christmas
And money is tight
I live on disability
It's cold tonight

My niece and great-nephew
Will be here next week
He's a growing child
More mouths to feed

Politicians in DC
Make more money than most
Get better benefits
The poor are their host

A Call to Contemplation

So why are tax dollars
Spent to spy on the free
The NSA and CIA
Have more money than me

Millions and billions I'll never see
Buy weapons and drones
To kill innocent people
And children are left in poverty

How much does it cost
To X-Ray everyone
Who flies on a plane
Nude files for what job?

Buildings are built
To house the unconstitutional
While there's no room in the shelters
And Snowden's exiled

Edward had more courage
Than any of you
Like Deep Throat before him
Did what he had to do

Deep Throat wasn't prosecuted
Too high up in the FBI
Snowden was a mere contractor
Who wouldn't tell a lie

Like many around me
I feel betrayed
Used and abused
By false promises made

And you with the salary
Pension and perks
Want all I have
Even though I can't work

Fix all these problems
You rich folk create
Expose the wrongdoings
And block the hate

But give any more
To half the source of it all?
I think not
Merry Christmas to all

*

703. For President Obama

For any federal employee
The mission is sacrosanct
First and above all else
Is the oath to defend and protect
The Constitution of the United States

Any nondisclosure agreement
Comes after taking the oath
The classified program was not created
To cover up the wrong-doing of most
Who have disregarded their oath

The Constitution prohibits
Inhibiting freedom of speech
By act of Congress
But they passed the PATRIOT Act anyway
Because they were afraid

A Call to Contemplation

"I know not what others may choose"
Patrick Henry once said
But he wasn't afraid of death
Unlike Congress who took an oath
To defend and protect

The President's oath is the same
As with all of the NSA
Yet no one's destroyed the ill-gotten gains
They argue about who will maintain
The files that defile the Constitution

None of them remember the mission
To protect and defend the Constitution
None of them is worthy to cast a stone
Against Ed Snowden
Who spoke out against all that's wrong

I didn't know when I voted for the President
"Transparent government" meant my life but not
    his
That "change" meant what's ok for me
Isn't good enough for the political rich
Who've committed treason

When the government overrides the Constitution
When the government demonizes its mission
Is there a country left in which I live?
I swore to defend the Constitution
But my words are my only weapon

*

704.

Fools place their trust
In gadgets and gizmos
They don't know what's inside
Or what's their true purpose

So much technology can help good people
It all had darker uses
So why let it fester?

Its sinister purpose
Will hurt more later
If you trust it

*

705.

Grief is the greatest of all pain
To feel loss and loneliness
And understand for whom you cared
Has left

But where?
It is not knowing
The veil over your eyes
That defines separation

The agony
Like one gone missing
Just not knowing
Sickens us with grief

It is no different
Than when a friend
Breaks the link
On which you depend

A Call to Contemplation

Some live on the surface
Aware only of what's in sight
While others have more depth
And perceive the shallow slight

Let go
You cannot hold them back
Nor want to
Cut the whole world slack

For no one wants to be chained
Those that would not stay
Would not good company make
So celebrate

Being wherever you are
Unafraid of turning a blind curve
Your journey is your own
Stay true to your way and don't swerve

*

706.

Illness brings pause
Consideration of all
We've contracted

An opportunity
To adjust direction
Change one's mind

Course corrections
Implementation
Requires breaking habits

But first one must stop
And take stock
Of being off path

Sickness stops
Sometimes death
To see where we're headed

And the rest
Is up to us
To use to reset

*

707.

I ventured out into the world
And encountered extreme hate
My perception of the world
Is bound to my emotional state
The pain I felt was personal
The pain I felt was great
The pain inflicted upon me
Led me to break

I was still inside the oven
When my soul snapped like a twig
One doesn't recover instantly
It takes support to mend
But instead I came to parents
Who weren't prepared and denied
The pain that I experienced
The reality I had died

A Call to Contemplation

And so I've lived with depression
That adults who knew me denied
I'd sleep away the extra hours
Or crawl in the closet and hide
An eleven year old tried
To commit suicide
But never talked about it
I was taught it's better to lie

It was considered an irreparable flaw
To feel the pain inside
We all have bodies made of nerves
But pain had to stay inside
So no one's allowed to scream for help
That's socially uncool
And to admit I wanted help
Would cast me outside my own world

People that make such rules
Are cold and empty and cruel
They think themselves capable
Of judging who is true
And they don't even know themselves
Because they only focus on details
And never see the big picture
They never see the whole person

Now I'm free from that awful system
That would have decided I wasn't as good
As I actually was because of my perception
Which couldn't be experienced
Without the false jabbing judgments
And misunderstanding of human emotions
As they relate to principles
I do not betray my values

Depression cannot be bought off
Nor bribed or blackmailed
But it can get pissed off
When the system fails
When those not depressed break the law
And hide behind position
When the Constitution is violated
And classified to cover wrong-doing

My disability pension
That I choose to live within
Is my only recompense
For not knowing I was depressed
The government games played with classified
Which was created to protect lives
Used only to cover up the crimes
Of sociopaths inside

The contractors rake in money
At taxpayers' expense
The politicians manipulate
At the direction of so-called defense
And everybody loses
The country divides itself
And all are offended
At unjust compilation of wealth

Meanwhile I now understand the source
Of my painful memories
I know watching girls my age being stabbed
Pushed me further from inner peace
Hate that brings violence is the ultimate illness
Depression is the result of being their victim
It is time for me to heal
It is time to leave that cold world

Politics and armies are frigid
They have no true creative potential
I will not take part again
Even if the world is at war
I am not at war with them
I will value each on his own merits
Regardless of partisanship
But no weapons

There I draw the line
As a victim of violence
I will defy them
From a distance
The warring will always find their fight
But I don't have to be part of it
I choose instead to write
And practice music

*

708.

 It doesn't happen quickly
The layers we put down
The threads that weave throughout our souls
Are along the threads of time wound

The daily patterns we take for granted
Are the essence of our souls
Record the past and predict the future
Even as we choose to grow

The courage to look in the mirror
To look oneself in the eye
Is no different from what is required
To consciously anticipate dying

Franki deMerle

For after death comes another day
Somewhere else or far away
But little changes
You are the same

*

709.

Security tries to define trustworthy
But one must first to be able to trust
Know its essence in front of your eyes

Security tries to define sound judgment
In a country of ridiculous mores
Based on false advertising

Security tries to define honesty
When it isn't honest with itself
It's a travesty

A true person knows vulnerability
As one of the risks of life
By which we learn individuality

Not everyone can be bribed
Or blackmailed or coerced
Not everyone is afraid of the truth

And they are the secure
Who do not trust the government
To tell the truth

*

710.

Leave me be to live my life
I vote my conscience
I speak out and write
I strive for harmony in my music

I want nothing to do
With us and them
Or false divisions
Or war

My life is about life
And love and kindness
I neither need nor want more

*

711.

Stop with the gossip
No more drama
If one must posit
Do so with caution

Do not disturb
Already still waters
The ripples you create
Will come back to haunt you

Memory is full of trauma
It's all in the past
But you cling to the drama
As if it's all you have

Everyone has their own—
They can't take care of
The problems you own
Because you choose to

We're but travelers
Passing through time
For a brief second
We keep what we find

*

712.

There are places we come to own
In our hearts
Places where the fog lifts
And shadows part
And we come into our own
Light and dark
In between
The wall and the art
Aware of neither
In our being

*

713.

The stillness of air
Stirred into noise
Whipping as wind
Unseen in poise

Senses by touch
All it touches is freshened
Or revealed for a moment
Uncovered

Quietly slips in and out
Or passes through reeds
In vibration
Or hidden deep in digestion

We focus on its sound
Without recognizing
We look at blood
Without seeing

*

714.

Prophets can predict
Because they understand
The nature of humans

If you look you can see
What will happen
Eventually

People are cruel
People are loud
People are animals

People are manipulated
In a crowd—
People are predictable

But some remain still
Some are quiet and listening
Some are kind

*

715.

Within the shelter
We don't see the Universe
We feel the cozy
Peaceful hearth

Which is the whole?
The vastness and wild
Or calm inner child
Neither

The world is a vessel
We live within
The body nestled
Within the din

To conceive of all
Without barrier
Unreal to the world
Which carries us

We think we are all
We are so much less

*

716.

Everyone is on their own journey
We rarely share it with them
They show us what we want to see
We crave distraction
We love to believe
We can judge them
So little we actually know

*

717.

When we are happy
When we are laughing
We are unaware
Of what is happening

We slip into a moment
A bubble of being
Rarely do we notice
Until it bursts

The opening, a gateway
Often we mistake
As important
A mere passing

Always with us
Always in us
Deeply recessed
Always peaceful

*

718.

Water everywhere nestled
Hidden within its vessels
In and out of my cells

The air is saturated
With water unseen
Glistening

In the corner of my eye
Hiding
Unbidden to cry

Franki deMerle

Step carefully
Where it reveals itself
Is slippery

*

719.

Many times I've fallen
Always a shock to the system
I trip myself up
And miss my own rhythm
Fall in slow motion
Look for ways
To break the momentum
Of the fall

Spare the hands
And land on my face
Protect the face
And the hand's in a brace
But unlike some
I don't heal completely
Scars are the wounds
The fibers replaced

Too many nerves
I have too much nerve
I have extra sensory perception
Throughout my body
You can't see it
But I feel it clearly

Take the wrong path
You stumble and fall
Wander off your own
At your own peril
It's important to know
For what you have come
Ignorance is the devil

*

720.

The mountain's enshrouded in fog
But I know it's there
I feel its presence
I breathe its air

Someday it will reveal itself
I'll be there
One with the mountain

*

721. Roundabout

Chilled salt air
A land still uplifting
Creation and death
The sea ever pounding
The past, the present
Interrupted before fulfilling

Franki deMerle

The car flipped over
Her head was spinning
Only one way out
Move on but remember
The ride isn't over
Stuck on the roundabout

Momentum keeps the top in spin
When it finally stops
We wind it up again
Spinning around we take it all in
The whole environment
Our unconscious takes in

Goal determines focus
Focus delivers perception
Which offers realization
And that changes everything we know
Moves our attention and changes our goals
And around we go

Like finds like
People are so different
So much is confusing
We cluster in comfort
With those most like
Ourselves and our comfort

Suck in the salt air
Wind in my hair
There is no confusion
Wind blows away delusion
Spins windmills producing power
To dance through life's most trying hours

A Call to Contemplation

A letter, word, sentence, book
Memories stirred up by a look
Surprises at every turn
But life in a straight line
Would be boringly undeserved
So we try one more time

The melody leads
The rhythm of breath
Vibrations of the soul condensed
Coda at the end
Starts all over again
Notes interwoven

Differences are aspects
Dimensions we forget
A bracelet to remember
With charms for each event
A band around the neck
For speech lest we forget

Life and death in circles
Spinning wheels we ride
One goes out with the tide
Lost to be unseen
Never knowing it will be our time
To meet with destiny

Air and water rule the stones
Air and water provide the fire
And life depends on all
Kindness and compassion are the stars
By which to navigate—
Never impulse and never hate

We catch ourselves in our own webs
And in struggling to be free
Cocoon ourselves in immobility
This isn't what life is supposed to be
Or is it?
Enough repeated
All else we forget

The wheel of fortune
Holds its secrets
Gravity recycled
Balancing efforts
Calm at the center
Of centrifugal force

The mystery of memory
The patterns that repeat
And have done so continually
Since the beginning of everything
We tread carefully
But we are all we see

*

722.

Things were not as I'd thought
But isn't this always true?
I was in hell
Where were you?

I don't like being connected
To ugliness out of control
I feel like it has left
A blemish on my soul

I will not be afraid
Of having met with the devil
I'm still real
But not evil

Life's purpose is not innocence
But conquering fear through peace
Not to hold on
But to release

*

723.

People get hurt
When they're not told the truth
When the facts are withheld
They're left out of the loop

Not to be thought of
Inflicts greater pain
Than even hate

Especially within family
It feels like shame
To be left out

A life once shared
Since extinguished
Over a month ago
Without being told

If I'd known
If I'd known where he lived
While he did
I could have called

But I wasn't part
Of my family
I would have liked to talk to him
I would have liked to have known

I kept the channels open
Or so I'd thought
They never said he'd moved back
They never said he was sick again

How do you write to your family
And talk about everything but
What's important?

Was it intentional?
They didn't want me to know?
I wasn't considered close?
I didn't deserve to be told?

If there'd been no communication
A lot could simply be unexplained
But I received false communication
A big lie now causing such pain

So I won't try it again
They're intentions are clear
I'm nothing to them

Loveless family is the most painful of all
It comes at me from all directions
The connections tenuous and strained
Though I've tried to keep the channels open

I have four family members by blood
There are no others anymore
And those who have dissed me need come no
         closer
There's no answer for them at my door

A Call to Contemplation

I know he never forgot me
I don't know why they pushed me aside
But I'm tired of those who verbally espouse
    "Christian" values
For show, for ego, for pride

I'm hurting
I'm forgotten
I'm not wanted in their lives

If love was ever there
It had only to be expressed
If only anyone had cared

People get hurt
And never recover
The relationships denied them

I grieve for the deaths
Of all involved—
Every one of them

Family meant a lot to me
Because it was preciously scarce
Family means nothing to shallow people
Who don't reach beyond themselves

No one wants to be the one left out
No one wants to be forgotten
No one wants to be lied about behind their back
And know it's a loveless marking

Life seems to me now to be a pattern
Of being forgotten and unwanted
But patterns persist where still is doubt
I'd hoped to be remembered

Maybe even loved
Doesn't look like it's to turn out
I'd have to have loving people who care
Four family members left

When I die will my friends be told?
Will anyone want to know?
If so, will they be blown off
Like they aren't even loved?

People get hurt
By not being told

*

724.

Narcissism is solitary
It doesn't need or want me
Unless I happen to agree

But I don't need to emulate
Or concern myself with what isn't mine
I only need to live my life

There are many perspectives
In my world
One demanding all
Is an immature child

I have no children
I'm no surrogate parent
For one trapped in himself

Leave the stress and toxins
Far from me
I suffered it all enough as a child
But I grew up
Leave me be

*

725.

People have issues
I heal from my own
Others must choose to heal
Before another can help

I don't accept issues
Left on my doorstep
Sweep them off the porch
To mingle with dust in the air

They are not mine
They need not exist
If someone has a problem
There's no cause to project

I'm not a movie screen
Nor am I a drama queen
Take your issue to the mirror
To see it clearly

And don't bother me
Until you've identified
That part of yourself
Where it began inside

*

726.

Kindness does not
Seek fault
Kindness does not
Speak rudely
Kindness wants
To allow others cause
Kindness wants
To speak softly

*

727.

The surf pounds
In and out
Healing sounds
Rhythm and doubt

I watch the wave break
Histrionic displays stress
I watch it ride out
Dissipate with no crest

Sky over the shore
A person demands accord
There are no demands on the beach
Only all you can hear and see

One insists all must be one way
But the wind blows away
While the surf pounds the shore
Any way it pleases

A Call to Contemplation

Black and white
Night and day
Locked beliefs
Wash away

Holding tense and tight
Ready for a fight
Soft sand yields to salt water
As a gull takes flight

But formulas must define all
And only a few know the key
High above the gull calls to all
Any may stand on the beach

I watch the tide come and go
Surf's sound blocks intruding egos
I watch the sea and I know
I'm only a drop in the ocean

*

728.

It takes a lifetime to live a story
It takes time to write
Anything of meaning

To have time is to have a great friend
To pursue your passion
To be true

The brilliance of birds in knowing our souls
To have them as friends
The truth will be told

Nature and time are interwoven
The variations in generations
Insure collective memorization

*

729.

I do not control the pen
The words come from within
The entrance to the greater world
Where DNA twists and galaxies swirl

Such pettiness of the waking state
Who to judge and who to hate
So much time wasted
Unseen door faces

Count the syllables
Follow the rules
That don't apply
Once you step inside

Inside is bigger than outside
And everyone may enter
Likeable and unlikeable alike
Kindly leave the ego outside

*

730.

The emotionally immature
Have come out to play
All around the world
Demanding their way
Temper tantrums with weapons
And suicidal haze
The problem is so many
Are born all at one time
We see all the insanity
Our species has imbibed
Personal responsibility
Is required for inner peace
It doesn't come with executions
But forgiveness and release
Sigh
How long must we wait
For selfishness and greed
To realize they are what they hate?
And forgive themselves
Move on
And grow up

*

731.

An idealist
Is a depressed optimist
Living with disappointment

A cynic
Is a realist
Without hope

Franki deMerle

Moderation
Balance
What lies between

*

732.

May readers of these words
Find peace in their hearts
Trust in their community
And quiet in the streets

May bullets fall unpropelled
From the shelves of stores
May missiles fail to launch
And children laugh once more

No longer dressed with terror
To the point of inflicting it
On others
No preoccupation with fear

May saline waters not turn to acid
May starfish, dolphins and whales live well
Without sickening sonar buoys from hell
Destroying their health

May young people have hope
And paths they can follow
That take them where they need to be
May schools welcome talent instead of greed

May air be clean and a joy to breathe
May rain be gently refreshing
May seasons be clear
And sea level established

May energy from sun, air and water
Be in excess of any fires
May a person be free
To sit, read and relax

I beg for balance
Lack of extremes
I ask for kindness
And pray for relief

*

733.

Path made of stone
To make steps secure
Hard and unyielding
Heavy, unwieldy
Silent last word

*

734.

What is this rhythm within me?
The pounding of the seas
Thunder in the air and earth
Music and harmonies

A good book
Trees for shade
A clear brook
I've got it made

My work is my play
To be is my joy
Senses are for listening and learning
And clearing the soul

Franki deMerle

Will I pass eternity
Rhyming, writing, sharing?
Is there any other way to be?
I never will stop caring

One must be aware of all
To be a part of it
If one fills the inside with fantasy
There's nowhere left for eternity to fit

*

735.

Clear to the bottom
Nothing hidden
Waves and harmonics
Made by what stays
Obstacles slowly worn away

The branch of a tree
With no more leaves
Catches between two rocks
And the patterns made
By the motion of time
Are intricate but they fade

I'm here for the moment
Always
Seeking peace
But never quiet
The sound of cascades

To be as clear
As what is before me
The element of which I'm made

*

736.

Dizziness more frequent
Direction confusion
This body almost spent
Staying in the present moment
I'll find my way yet

*

737.

I pity the person of anger
For anger blocks all true emotion
When angry you cannot know
What you're feeling

But sitting calmly
Or sleeping and dreaming
You are your feelings
They're overwhelming

I love the way different languages
Allow for different expression
And different views of perception
Of being

It is worth knowing at least two
If ever you are to know you
There must be dimension
Created by alternate perception

*

Franki deMerle

738. Lucia

Water falling over rocks
Foamy and white and energized
Moving patterns of the pool
Moving along
Aerated and cool

The illusion of waterfalls
It is always there
But in motion
The truth of the waterfall
Is it is forever new

*

739.

The silver sliver of a crescent moon
Boldly glows into my bedroom
Without shame frames itself in my window
As if it has forgotten how little shows

But it cares not with confidence
For it is whole while so much bleak
It does not care what I see of it
It is where it is meant to be

*

740.

The human body is complex
A layer of skin so very thin
To protect within
A sheer membrane
A covering of vulnerability
A recipient of so little pleasure
Amidst so much pain
Easily torn away
Skin bears the scars
Reminder marks
Life ciphers

*

741. for Vaughn

Death comes to all
The painful transformation
Of being born to a new family
Of having to trust them
To take care of your needs

Marines go to battle
Assuming they've already died
Living the last act
If not heroic they tried
Killed by their own

A country screams about the offenses
Of which it is most guilty
Agent Orange versus weapons of destruction
Cruelty to veterans versus human rights
With an arsenal of nuclear weapons

Franki deMerle

We are the evil in which we live
We'd rather judge than learn to forgive
Fold a flag when somebody dies
Say what a good person and say goodbye
And forget

I won't forget you
You chose one hell over another
Left racism and hate for the jungle
Somebody else's civil war
And now it's almost over

I escaped both
The confederates and jungle war
I live a few years more
As a witness to those I've lost
To the egos of temporary government personnel

We're forced to elect them
We never like them
They never represent us
It's just a corporate exercise
In foolishness

National pride—what's that?
Separating us from them
Enabling differences
Ignoring likeness
Killing ourselves

Because we are one planet
An attack on one is on all
Interceding in another's war is hubris
Misguided testosterone
The capital venture club

Life is painful
So much loss for no reason
All the Gitas and Bibles can't explain them
Or why it hurt so much
To lose a friend

*

742.

Why have I known so many mean people?
Why was my mother so quick to play tricks on me?
Why did she enjoy stabbing me in the back?

I have closer relationships with animals
I find joy of living in flowers
But I see Nature's suffering

To live in peace one has to forget
Everything bad outside your little piece of
happiness
But I see it

We have such a short window of opportunity
For finding and being ourselves
Before interference wrestles us

No matter how much mental discipline
Everything dissipates in the end
We have to start again

*

Franki deMerle

743.

On the lake trail
Many wildflowers smile
My heartbeat slows
Allows me to rest in the moment
Needles of the past pass through
Into the abyss they fall

Patterns are the flowers of my notes
Every phrase a breath of cool air
Hearing my own sighs and moans
Mix in and out of my soul
And float
Yet another breath billows

Heavy—no, light—no, weightless
Under the sky above the lake
Nowhere else to be
Gaitless and free

*

744.

A life without kindness
Is unimaginable horror
But easily corrected
If kindness is learned

It needn't be seen or heard
It can be found
Known
Shared all around

No need for self-pity
Or anger or violence
Just a little kindness
Makes life worth living

*

745.

Your songs were cryptic
I was fooled at first
But not for long

I'm a sucker for clues
Defining a mystery
I love a good song

But the truth lies within
And in the exterior life
They must intertwine

You reached so deep
Into the collective
Where we all are a piece

You've a sense of class
I break barriers where I can
An illusion of glass

You discriminate
Where I want to educate
Against social bias

Franki deMerle

I never want to live like you
Unless you become enlightened
I only wish you'd follow your own clues

*

746.

The tall ones view us like bugs
An infestation short on cooperation
Some practice destruction
Some pollination
We cut some down
And enjoy others' shade
But we are not like them
Standing and being
Watching and seeing
They preceded us here
Hopefully to remain

*

747.

The wonder of it all
Fire, water, air
Waves of sound and light
This life gives us place

Location, location
Here is where we are
While dreaming of everywhere
We are set in motion

Here we are particle
In a specific spot
Cross over to be wave and space
The common thread is thought

A Call to Contemplation

Silver thread within the shell
The body breaks in which we dwell
And we are free in space
With no sense of place

Look to your body
You'll wear it out soon enough
Look to your thoughts
And all is enough

*

748.

We're here to learn
To live with pain
The secret's no secret
But painfully gained

We think of ourselves
We focus on pain
We get lost in ourselves
Which creates more pain

It's simple enough
To look around
To learn to cope
With others around

By smiling and cheering
Them on in their trials
Do what we can
Having fun all the while

Because isolation
Unless enlightened
Dwells on itself
And forgets all else

See the big picture
Enjoy the view
Don't get lost in detail
Get lost in the view

*

749.

Fears continue until understood
From death or childhood
Suppressed so we could
Continue living
Day to day crises
Bombardments, interruptions
We make time for ease
Must make time to see
The moment, the present
Clean the slate
Learn to forgive
The key is forgiveness
Before we can live
To face the past
Which—make no mistake—
Will repeat till remembered
However long it takes

*

750. for Robin Williams

So many things I'd never thought of
You spouted naturally
At a speed most can't keep up with
You let it all flow free

A Call to Contemplation

You were the epitome of human being
Kindness incarnate
Not making fun of others
But of life for us to laugh

The clown crying inside
Some mock the creative fire
That enlightens and consumes us
As we forgive them and reach higher

It hurts to live with cruelty
What about this life is not?
Kindness laughing freely
I hope that's what you've got

I choose to live in a place
With legal death with dignity
You chose your time and way
Someday we'll all be free

Gentle spirit, judge me not
As I will not judge you
Smile now and forever, my friend
That's how I'll remember you

*

751.

Unable to digest
Stuck
Can't move on
Obstacle I've been going around
Getting bigger
Stops me from traveling and getting around
Keeps me stuck at home

Franki deMerle

Can't keep up with what I'm not supposed to eat
Don't know anymore how much to eat
Feel like I've failed my body

Trouble remembering what meds to take
No longer have control over fibromyalgia pain
Bones no longer get meds to strengthen
Not absorbing enough electrolytes
Have become self-absorbed

Don't know what to do
Weak
Blocked
Rot
Decay
Death is nature's way of telling us to slow down
Withdraw
Humiliated
I can't live like this

One more day before flush out
Fluids till x-ray
Thursday I find out if I get my life back

More exercise
Less waiting
Less late eating

Food is not my friend
No sense trying to be around other people
They want to tell you what to do without knowing
That causes hurt

A Call to Contemplation

Never discuss food, health, or politics with
ANYONE
I'm not a body people want to be around
Stop calling people
They're not interested in me or this problem
They just want to think they can solve everything

Let go of the world
Everything's slowed down
One breath at a time
Breathe instead of act
Breathe instead of eat

How can I take good care of Chiana and Kiko
When I don't know how to take care of myself?
If I can't live independently
I don't want to

I did what the specialist said and it made everything
worse
Then he didn't even care
I was different so he's done with me

I'm different
Others don't identify with me
Stupid to keep writing
Just fodder for people to laugh at
I've never had writers block
So I got this instead to stop me
Drawing is best

*

Franki deMerle

752.

The older I get
The less I care
For politics, religion
And other peoples' affairs

Those who choose to fight
Can do so without me
No one is right
It's just what they believe

Even the old-fashioned
Concept of karma
No longer rings true
It's all too much drama

I live for the music
For the air we all breathe
For hugs and for smiles
And for quiet company

But never for power
And never for profit
Business is sour
And I don't like it

Keep the drama
Nature is plenty for me
Of color and beauty
I'll just add music

*

753.

Life is short and full of pain
Full of joy that cannot sustain
Let go of it all and go between

The arts connect us to the universe
The arts connect us to ourselves
The path lies within the self

It's not found in business
Or in careers or in fear
It's always with us

But the brain has to tune
Into the body central
To feel what is real
All those opinions and judgments
Are external and go nowhere
You can't get there by scheming and plotting

The emotion of joy is pain
The feeling of pain is joy
They lead inside just the same

Art is a way of finding the path
Following it home
To the real world

*

754.

Rare moments of clarity
Awareness of Nature's beauty
New for the first time and ancient
Daunting in vastness and changes
Overwhelmed by peace rather than crises
Melting the painful, frozen depression

All it's about is the calm neural path
Connected to Nature and within
Tuning out the nonsense without
Senses make sense when channeled naturally

Obstacles are potential viewpoints
For seeing beyond the world of fads

Kindness is more permanent than that
It's all about permanent inner peace
No more drama please
Don't try to provoke or prove anything
No details are important
Except in beauty
Sensuality exists for spirituality
Simplicity is the best policy

*

755.

My thoughts are my own
No one else's
They tell me how to feel
Thoughts control
And emotions steer the wheel

Feelings must be put aside
To see that what I think is mine
Feelings express the body's inside
But thoughts are formed beyond
Thinking I am worthless
Is not the body's fault

I must see the thoughts behind
The feelings controlling me
To know just how to change my mind
To leave behind suffering

*

756.

Life is hard enough in this world
Confusion of body, emotions and thoughts
Without adding a virtual universe
For business, taxes and such

It stabs at me from every direction
The hate and falsity
Bring back natural beauty please
Harmony is a basic need

*

757.

Being sensitive is now considered an illness
But it doesn't cause suffering
That's perception and there's a big difference

I have both
I can't always cope with artificiality
But I cope with Nature and harmony

Money's artificial—a fictional thing
I've learned to manage
But not with dishonesty

And I express myself verbally
I even have a blog
I will never leave quietly

I contemplate my weakness and strength
And find duplicity succumbs
Into one

One that perceives and speaks
One that feels and sees
One that knows what is real

Delusions of profit and judgment
Dissipate at the voice of music
To reveal feelings and poetry

Most of the world rejects all that I am
Through violence, hatred and lack of emotion
But there is always a place for me

*

758.

Fog settles in among the firs
A lone horse grazes
Enjoying his blanket of privacy
On the edge of two plates colliding
On the little water planet

Elephants are dying
They've given us sounds of joy
Rolling arpeggios of short stringed ivory
Lifting emotions beyond the range of sound
Joyful crying

Fog settles among my thoughts
A lone soul embracing
Enjoying the notes from my fingers and ears
My harp has no ivory
Joyfully trying

To practice my practice as I practice
Oblivious to all else
Music is language communicating
Blocking the pain signals
Just the essence of self

*

759.

Trust in what is
Trust isn't easy in this life
But trust binds atoms
And overcomes others' spite

Franki deMerle

Trust the present
To reveal a surprise
And leave the untrusted
Behind

I've trusted a country
But it didn't need me
I've trusted people
That didn't trust me

I've trusted my dreams
They shape reality
I trust in the present
It's where I'll always be

I trust simplicity
Life's too complicated
Too much technology
Is overrated

I trust in souls
Who dream with me
To share oneself completely
Is the essence of trusting

Thought precedes feeling
We choose what we think
I think of you often
I feel your presence

This life's been a lesson for both of us
Twin soul polar opposites so much alike
The paradox of time
We can't be side by side

A Call to Contemplation

We've both tried
We only dream together
As waves not particles
As waves we fly

So closely circling
Each other's orbit
So close to touching
We just have to trust

I always trust you
Yes, it's reality
We're always connected
But never seen

I have a good life
You seem to be happy
Yes, we dreamed together
Please trust me

Your singing makes me happy
I know now that it's you
And I am listening
To you

*

760.

I tried resisting those dreams long ago
They were just dreams after all
But so much more

You're very persistent
I love to listen
I love it when we dream together

Franki deMerle

And none of this matters
The pains of the world
Because it's all matter

I play with words
Words play with our minds
It's just better when they rhyme

And you're playing in my old neighborhood
Like our waking worlds are coming together
I feel it all coming closer

You're a ray of starshine
The voice of hope
The love of my life

That goes so far beyond
My little mind
Beyond all I know

For me dreams have always been a gift
For me they guide my way
We've come a long, long way

Maybe it's now the Age of Aquarius
Maybe I've finally healed from the past
Maybe we're coming together at last

*

761.

I've tried for decades to find the word
That describes our relationship
I've been through the list
None seem to fit

I was confused for so very long
And then it came to me in an instant
I am your muse

*

762.

It doesn't matter what you believe
To experience an alternate perspective
Gives depth to your being

*

763. Roundabout Part 2

Simple expectations
Run into complications
Searching for the pieces
We run around in circles
En todo es uno
If we could only see it

Are memories reliable?
Everything's always changing
And yet we crave a solid past
The brain expects
Concrete facts
Myths of reality

The hands move round the clock each day
Déjà vu, habit and running away
Time is the chain
Work or play
Dive deep within
And lead your own way

Franki deMerle

A circular puzzle
The pieces all curve
Straight lines in Nature
Are mostly vertical
We bend and we twist
But slowly we learn

You have to know the lay of the land
To know when to turn
To get off the circle
A choice is required to get anywhere
A commitment to learn
What really matters

A Mobius strip
An infinity sign
Life with a twist
The roller coaster climbs
And always ends
At the starting line

You can't research the future
You cannot trust the past
To not be misrepresented
We take history for granted
But should we?

One may tread lightly
Avoiding the stickiness
Careful to be still
Commotion attracts attention
Makes us lose our balance
And start all over again

A Call to Contemplation

In stillness is escape
In the moment quiet
Long enough the web disintegrates
There is nothing to fear
We've started over so many times
But now we're here

*

Appendix

INDEX of Poem's first line and Poem number

Appendix

Appendix

Appendix

Appendix

Appendix

About the Author

Franki deMerle grew up in Huntsville, Alabama, during the 1960s and '70s, and her experiences are the basis for the novel, Deception Past. deMerle's name is on the Wall of Tolerance at the Southern Poverty Law Center in Montgomery, Alabama. She is a founding member of the Build the Dream Foundation, which built the memorial to Rev. Dr. Martin Luther King Jr. in Washington, DC. deMerle is also the author of Ripples on the Surface, a collection of poetry written 1969-2006. The author's proceeds from the first edition, Ripples on the Surface went directly to Global Partners for Development to help women with HIV/AIDS in Uganda start their own businesses. Proceeds from subsequent editions go to a retired school teacher. deMerle now lives in the Pacific Northwest, where she continues to write poetry and reincarnation-related novels. "You don't have to believe in reincarnation (though many do) to enjoy a novel any more than you have to believe in aliens from outer space (who knows for sure?) to enjoy science fiction." Her website is www.reincarnationbooks.com.